Fishing
With
Granddaddy B

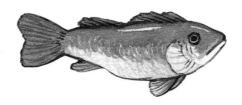

Fishing With Granddaddy B

ISBN 0-687-02570-2

Printed in Hong Kong

02 03 04 05 06 07 08 09 10 11 – 10 9 8 7 6 5 4 3 2 1

Abingdon Press • Nashville

Fishing
With
Granddaddy B

Tony Pennington

Illustrated by Jennifer Emery

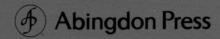

Abingdon Press

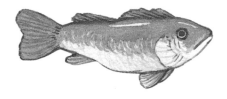

Dedication

❋❋❋❋❋

**In honor of
L. B. (Granddaddy B) Newsome
and Eva B. Newsome**

**For my girls:
Torrie, Taryn, Toni, and Tia**

Red had a difficult time getting to sleep. Tomorrow was a special day. He was going fishing with his grandfather.

Red was the nickname his grandmother gave him. She said that in the summertime the sunshine made his skin look red.

Early the next morning Grandma woke Red up. "Get up, Red. It is time to go fishing," she said.

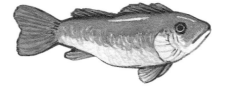

8

Red got dressed and ran downstairs.

Grandma had grits, eggs, and bacon on the table. Red thought Grandma was the best cook in the whole world. Before he started to eat, Red bowed his head to say grace.

"Thank you, God, for this food. In Jesus' name, Amen."

Grandma smiled. She was glad Red knew how important it is to give thanks to God.

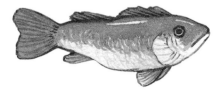

10

Just as Red finished his breakfast, Granddaddy B came inside.

Red called his grandfather Granddaddy B. He did not know why, he just always had.

Granddaddy B had been putting the fishing rods into the truck. "It is time to go, Red," his grandfather said.

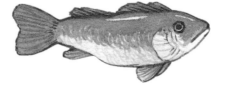

ed gave Grandma a big hug and a kiss, then he ran to the truck. He jumped into the truck and buckled his seat belt. It was time to go fishing!

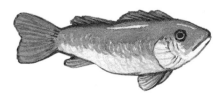

14

Granddaddy B, why is it still dark outside?"

"It is five o'clock in the morning," Granddaddy B replied. "We must get to the lake early while the fish are still hungry."

"What kind of fish will we catch?" Red asked.

"We will catch some catfish and crappie."

"Will we use mice to catch the catfish?" Red asked.

"No," his grandfather laughed. "We will use worms."

The lake was far away from the city. They passed a farm and saw some horses and some cows. At another farm they saw pigs and lots of chickens.

At last they arrived at the lake. "This looks like the perfect spot," said Granddaddy B.

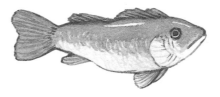

18

Granddaddy B helped Red put a worm on the hook. "What is that red and white ball on the line for?" Red asked.

"That is called a bobber," his grandfather said. "When it goes under the water there will be a fish on the line."

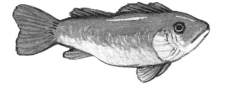

Red kept his eye on the bobber.

Suddenly the bobber went under the water. "I got one! I got one!" Red shouted.

His grandfather said, "Don't let him get away!"

22

Red held up the fish he had caught. He had the biggest smile on his face that Grandma had ever seen.

Granddaddy B and Red were tired and decided to go to bed early. Red took a bath and changed into his pajamas. Before climbing into bed he knelt down to say his prayers. "Now I lay me down to sleep. I pray the Lord my soul to keep. Before I sleep I want to say, thank you, God, for another blessed day."

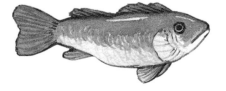

Red went to sleep with a big smile on his face. He had caught his first fish, but best of all he had spent the day with his Granddaddy B.